Dive into the vibrant world of 1980's cinema with our ultimate movie trivia book!

Packed with 101 questions, this meticulously crafted collection captures the essence of a decade that redefined Hollywood.

From blockbuster hits like "E.T. the Extra-Terrestrial" and "Back to the Future" to cult classics like "The Goonies" and "Ferris Bueller's Day Off," this book challenges your knowledge and brings back the magic of the 80's.

Whether you're a die-hard film buff or a casual moviegoer, our trivia book offers hours of nostalgic fun, perfect for parties, family gatherings, or solo entertainment.

Relive the iconic moments, memorable quotes, and unforgettable characters that made the 80's an unparalleled era in movie history!

E.T. THE EXTRA-TERRESTRIAL (1982)

WHAT IS THE NAME OF THE YOUNG BOY WHO
BEFRIENDS THE ALIEN IN THIS MOVIE?

ANSWER: ELLIOTT

THE BREAKFAST CLUB (1985)

WHAT ARE THE FIVE MAIN CHARACTERS'
NAMES WHO SPEND DETENTION
TOGETHER IN THIS FILM?

ANSWER: ANDREW, BRIAN, CLAIRE,
ALLISON, AND JOHN.

BACK TO THE FUTURE (1985)

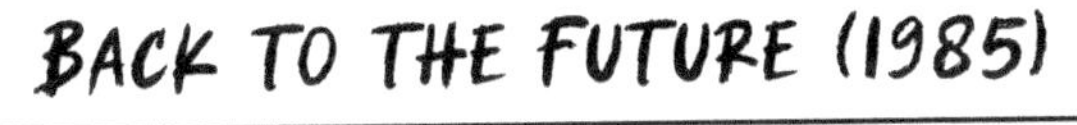

WHAT IS THE NAME OF THE
TIME MACHINE IN THIS MOVIE?

ANSWER: DELOREAN.

RAIDERS OF THE LOST ARK (1981)

WHO PLAYS THE ICONIC ARCHAEOLOGIST INDIANA JONES IN THIS FILM?

ANSWER: HARRISON FORD.

GHOSTBUSTERS (1984)

WHAT IS THE NAME OF THE GIANT
MARSHMALLOW MAN THAT APPEARS
IN THE CLIMAX OF THIS FILM?

ANSWER: STAY PUFT MARSHMALLOW MAN.

The Shining (1980)

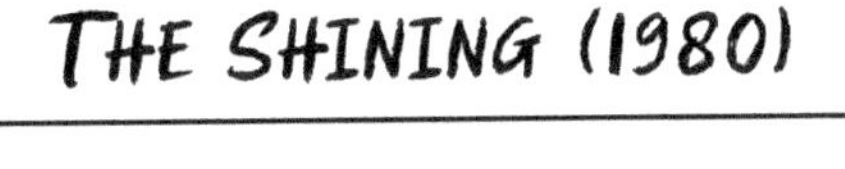

What famous phrase is repeatedly typed by Jack Torrance in this film?

ANSWER: "ALL WORK AND NO PLAY
MAKES JACK A DULL BOY."

TOP GUN (1986)

WHAT IS THE CALL SIGN OF THE FILM'S
PROTAGONIST, PLAYED BY TOM CRUISE?

ANSWER: MAVERICK.

Ferris Bueller's Day Off (1986)

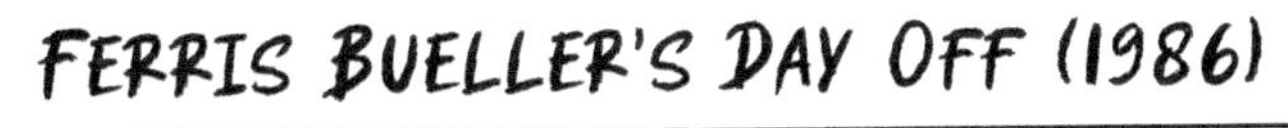

What is the name of Ferris Bueller's best friend in the film?

ANSWER: CAMERON FRYE.

The Empire Strikes Back (1980)

Who reveals the famous line, "I am your father," in this Star Wars sequel?

ANSWER: DARTH VADER.

THE PRINCESS BRIDE (1987)

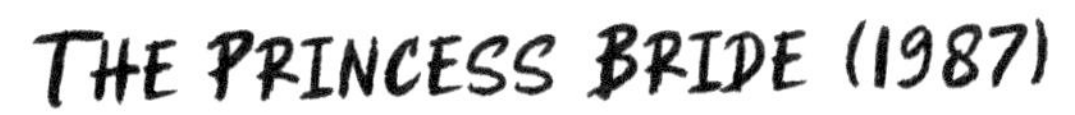

WHAT IS THE CATCHPHRASE REPEATED
THROUGHOUT THE FILM BY INIGO MONTOYA?

ANSWER: "HELLO. MY NAME IS INIGO MONTOYA.
YOU KILLED MY FATHER. PREPARE TO DIE."

Die Hard (1988)

What is the name of the protagonist played by Bruce Willis in this action film?

ANSWER: JOHN MCCLANE.

THE GOONIES (1985)

WHAT IS THE NAME OF THE PIRATE WHOSE
TREASURE THE KIDS ARE SEARCHING
FOR IN THIS ADVENTURE FILM?

Answer: One-Eyed Willy.

BEETLEJUICE (1988)

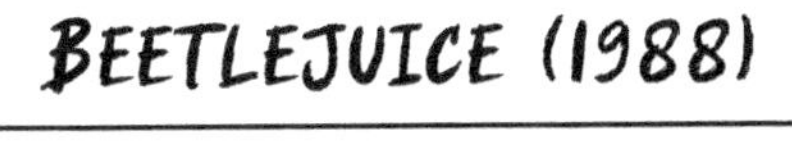

WHO DO THE MAITLANDS, THE GHOSTLY
PROTAGONISTS, HIRE TO SCARE AWAY
THE LIVING IN THEIR HOUSE?

ANSWER: BEETLEJUICE.

THE TERMINATOR (1984)

WHO PLAYS THE TITULAR ROLE OF THE
TERMINATOR IN THIS SCI-FI THRILLER?

ANSWER: ARNOLD SCHWARZENEGGER.

BLADE RUNNER (1982)

WHAT IS THE TERM USED FOR THE
HUMAN-LIKE ROBOTS IN THIS
DYSTOPIAN FUTURE FILM?

Answer: Replicants.

STAND BY ME (1986)

WHAT ARE THE FOUR BOYS SEARCHING FOR ON THEIR JOURNEY IN THIS COMING-OF-AGE FILM?

ANSWER: A DEAD BODY.

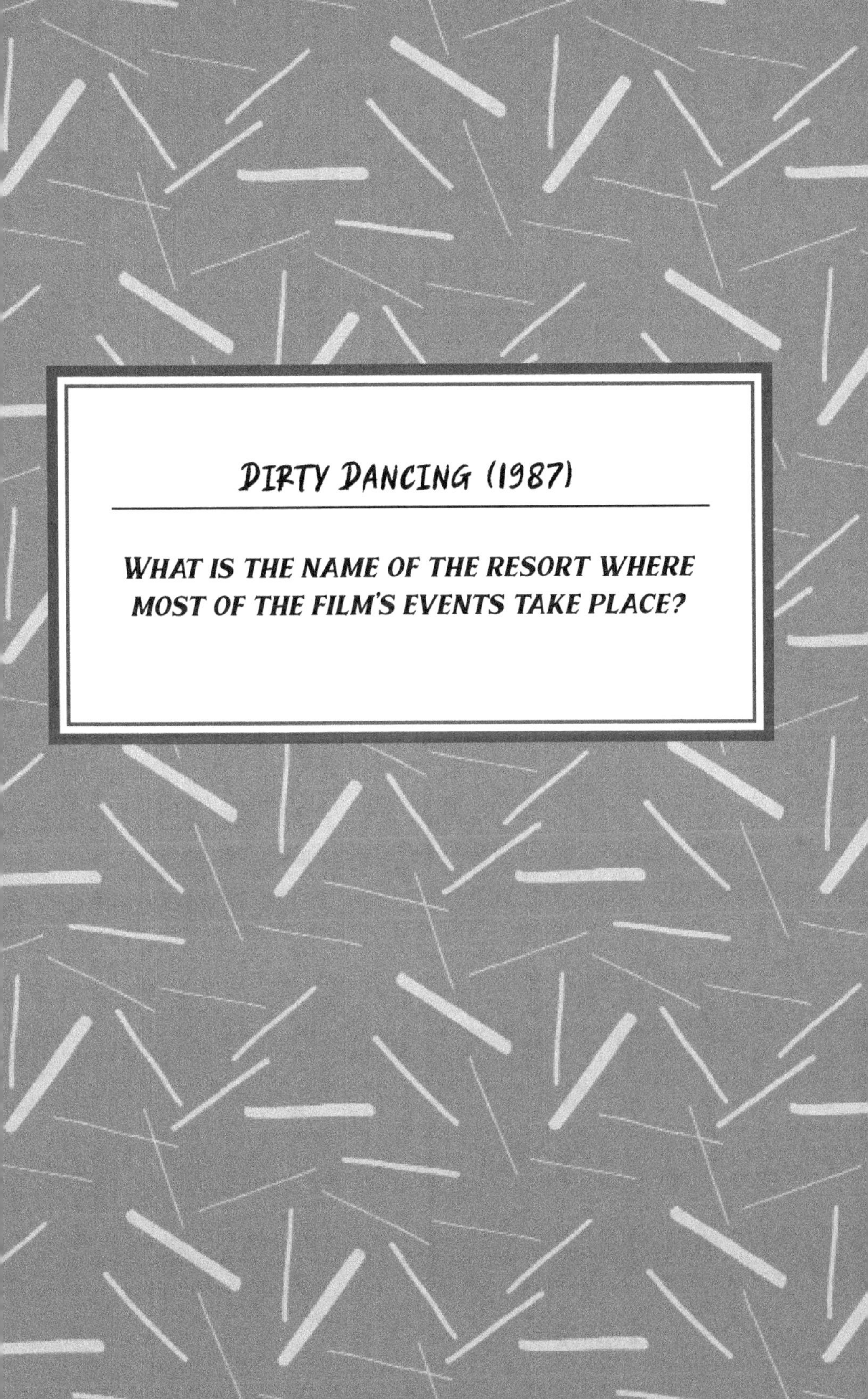

DIRTY DANCING (1987)

WHAT IS THE NAME OF THE RESORT WHERE MOST OF THE FILM'S EVENTS TAKE PLACE?

ANSWER: KELLERMAN'S.

THE KARATE KID (1984)

WHO TAKES DANIEL UNDER HIS WING TO
TEACH HIM THE DISCIPLINE OF KARATE?

Answer: Mr. Miyagi

THE LOST BOYS (1987)

WHAT IS THE NAME OF THE COASTAL TOWN WHERE THIS FILM'S VAMPIRE STORY UNFOLDS?

ANSWER: *SANTA CARLA.*

A NIGHTMARE ON ELM STREET (1984)

WHO IS THE SUPERNATURAL VILLAIN IN THIS HORROR FILM WHO HAUNTS TEENAGERS' DREAMS?

ANSWER: FREDDY KRUEGER.

ROCKY III (1982)

WHAT IS THE NICKNAME OF ROCKY'S OPPONENT, CLUBBER LANG, IN THIS FILM?

ANSWER: THE SOUTHSIDE SLUGGER.

The Untouchables (1987)

Who plays the role of the legendary lawman Eliot Ness in this crime drama?

ANSWER: KEVIN COSTNER.

The Empire Strikes Back (1980)

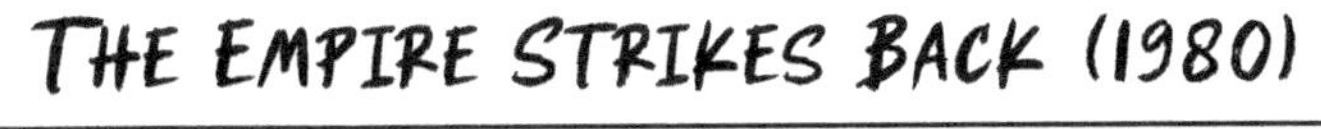

WHAT IS THE NAME OF THE BOUNTY HUNTER WHO CAPTURES HAN SOLO AND BRINGS HIM TO JABBA THE HUTT?

ANSWER: BOBA FETT.

THE OUTSIDERS (1983)

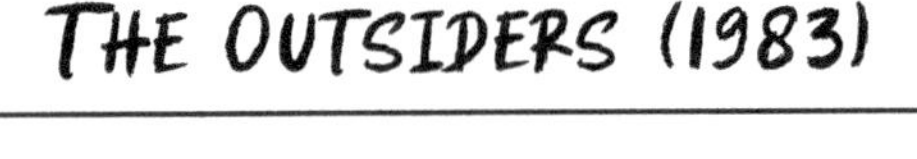

WHAT IS THE NAME OF THE RIVAL GANG
IN THIS FILM, WHOSE MEMBERS INCLUDE
JOHNNY AND DALLAS?

*ANSWER: THE SOCS
(PRONOUNCED "SO-SHES").*

An American Werewolf in London (1981)

WHAT IS THE CHARACTER'S NAME WHO
TRANSFORMS INTO A WEREWOLF
DURING A FULL MOON?

ANSWER: DAVID KESSLER.

RAIN MAN (1988)

WHO PLAYS THE CHARACTER RAYMOND BABBITT, AN AUTISTIC SAVANT, IN THIS FILM?

ANSWER: DUSTIN HOFFMAN

LABYRINTH (1986)

WHO STARS AS SARAH, A YOUNG GIRL WHO MUST NAVIGATE A FANTASTICAL LABYRINTH TO RESCUE HER BROTHER?

ANSWER: JENNIFER CONNELLY.

Stand and Deliver (1988)

What subject does the dedicated teacher Jaime Escalante teach to underprivileged students in this film?

ANSWER: MATHEMATICS.

Terms of Endearment (1983)

What is the name of Emma and Aurora's close friend, played by Jack Nicholson?

ANSWER: GARRETT BREEDLOVE.

The Color Purple (1985)

Who directed this film adaptation of Alice Walker's novel, which explores the life of Celie Harris?

ANSWER: Steven Spielberg.

Planes, Trains and Automobiles (1987)

What two actors play the mismatched travel companions, Neal Page and Del Griffith?

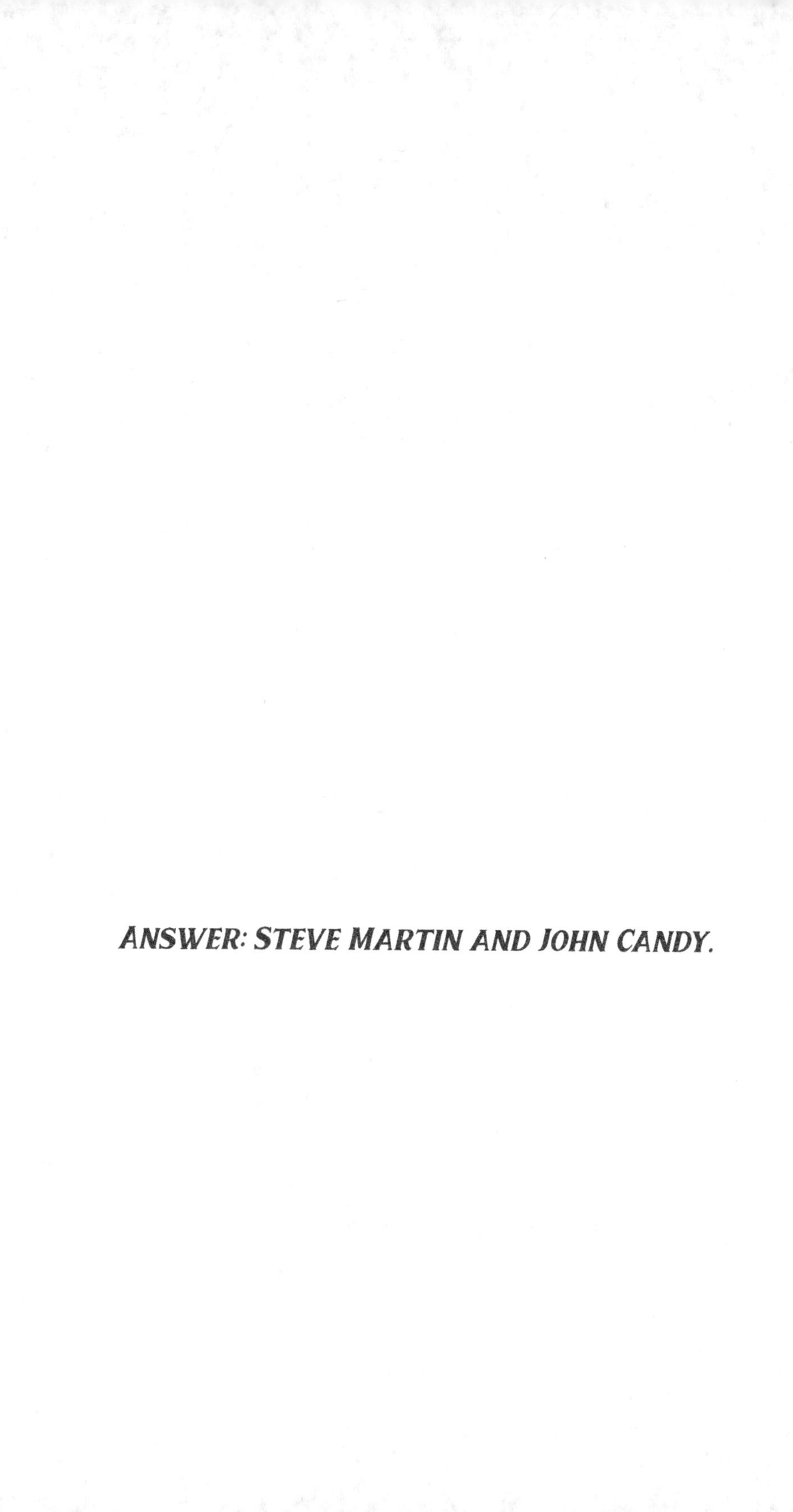
ANSWER: STEVE MARTIN AND JOHN CANDY.

9 TO 5 (1980)

WHO LEADS A GROUP OF OFFICE WORKERS IN SEEKING REVENGE AGAINST THEIR SEXIST BOSS IN THIS COMEDY?

ANSWER: JANE FONDA.

RISKY BUSINESS (1983)

WHAT DOES JOEL GOODSEN'S FRIEND MILES
ENCOURAGE HIM TO TURN HIS HOUSE
INTO WHEN HIS PARENTS ARE AWAY?

ANSWER: A BROTHEL.

FULL METAL JACKET (1987)

WHAT IS THE NICKNAME GIVEN TO
THE BRUTAL DRILL INSTRUCTOR
PLAYED BY R. LEE ERMEY?

ANSWER: GUNNY.

The Neverending Story (1984)

What is the name of the magical land that Bastian discovers in a mysterious book?

ANSWER: FANTASIA.

Romancing the Stone (1984)

What is the profession of the protagonist, Joan Wilder, in this adventure-comedy?

ANSWER: SHE'S A ROMANCE NOVELIST.

FIRST BLOOD (1982)

WHAT IS THE NICKNAME OF THE
VIETNAM WAR VETERAN AND FORMER
GREEN BERET WHO BATTLES LAW
ENFORCEMENT IN THIS FILM?

ANSWER: RAMBO.

E.T. THE EXTRA-TERRESTRIAL (1982)

WHAT IS THE FAMOUS LINE E.T. SAYS WHEN HE WANTS TO CONTACT HIS HOME PLANET?

ANSWER: "E.T. PHONE HOME."

THE LITTLE MERMAID (1989)

WHAT IS THE NAME OF ARIEL'S FISH FRIEND WHO ACCOMPANIES HER ON HER ADVENTURES?

ANSWER: FLOUNDER.

DIE HARD (1988)

WHAT IS THE NAME OF THE TERRORIST
LEADER WHO TAKES EVERYONE HOSTAGE?

ANSWER: HANS GRUBER.

PLATOON (1986)

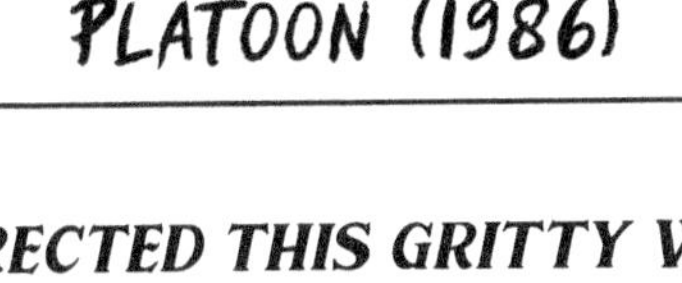

WHO DIRECTED THIS GRITTY WAR FILM
SET DURING THE VIETNAM WAR?

ANSWER: OLIVER STONE.

Trading Places (1983)

What do the wealthy Duke brothers bet on, leading to the switch between Louis Winthorpe III and Billy Ray Valentine?

ESCAPE FROM NEW YORK (1981)

WHAT ICONIC ACTOR PORTRAYS THE EYE-PATCHED ANTIHERO SNAKE PLISSKEN IN THIS DYSTOPIAN ACTION FILM?

Answer: Kurt Russell.

FIELD OF DREAMS (1989)

IN WHAT CROP DOES RAY KINSELLA CARVE
A BASEBALL FIELD IN THIS FANTASY DRAMA?

ANSWER: CORN.

Beverly Hills Cop (1984)

What actor plays the street-smart
Detroit cop Axel Foley in
this action-comedy?

ANSWER: EDDIE MURPHY.

FLASHDANCE (1983)

WHAT IS THE MAIN CHARACTER
ALEX OWENS' DREAM OCCUPATION IN
THIS DANCE-CENTRIC FILM?

ANSWER: SHE WANTS TO BE A
PROFESSIONAL DANCER.

ROBOCOP (1987)

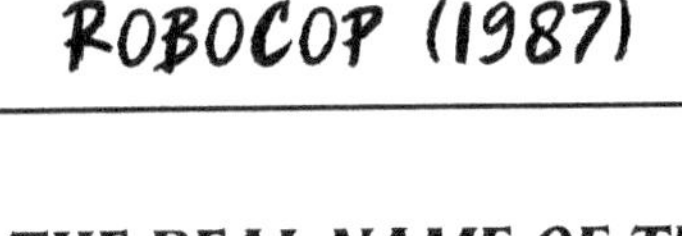

WHAT IS THE REAL NAME OF THE POLICE OFFICER WHO BECOMES THE CYBORG CRIMEFIGHTER IN THIS SCI-FI FILM?

ANSWER: ALEX MURPHY.

BIG (1988)

HOW DOES 12-YEAR-OLD JOSH BASKIN
MAGICALLY TRANSFORM INTO AN
ADULT IN THIS COMEDY?

ANSWER: HE MAKES A WISH ON A CARNIVAL
FORTUNE-TELLING MACHINE.

THE FLY (1986)

WHO STARS AS THE SCIENTIST SETH BRUNDLE, WHO UNDERGOES A HORRIFYING TRANSFORMATION IN THIS SCI-FI HORROR?

ANSWER: JEFF GOLDBLUM.

THE KILLING FIELDS (1984)

IN WHAT COUNTRY DOES MOST OF THE
FILM'S STORY TAKE PLACE DURING
THE KHMER ROUGE REGIME?

ANSWER: CAMBODIA.

GHOSTBUSTERS (1984)

WHAT IS THE NAME OF THE GHOST THAT THE GHOSTBUSTERS FIRST CAPTURE IN THE HOTEL?

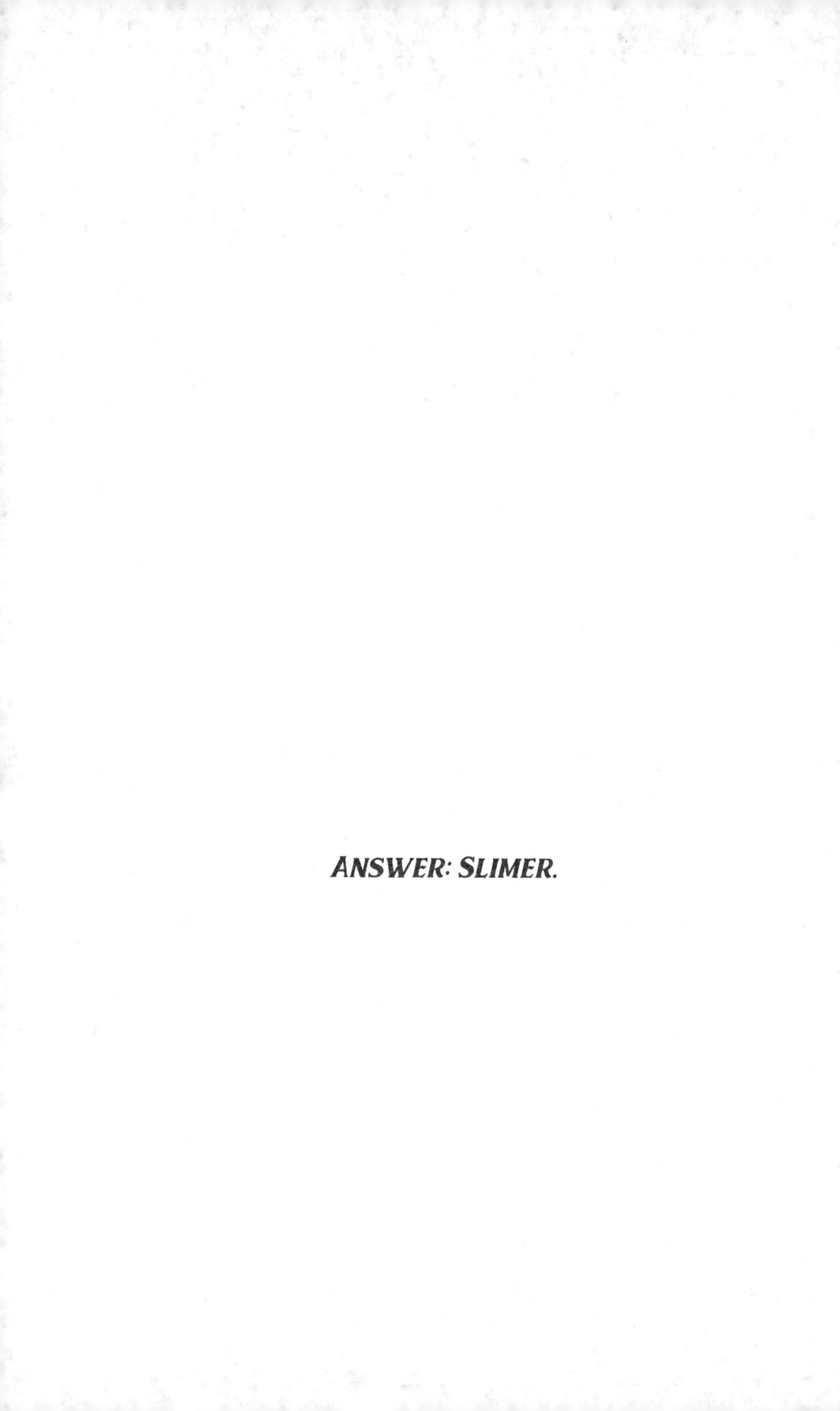

ANSWER: SLIMER.

BACK TO THE FUTURE (1985)

WHO IS THE MAIN ANTAGONIST THAT
BULLIES BOTH GEORGE MCFLY
AND MARTY MCFLY?

ANSWER: BIFF TANNEN.

The Karate Kid (1984)

What is the famous technique Mr. Miyagi teaches Daniel-san, involving waxing cars?

ANSWER: "WAX ON, WAX OFF".

PLANES, TRAINS, AND AUTOMOBILES (1987)

WHAT IS THE DESTINATION THAT
NEAL PAGE IS TRYING TO REACH FOR
THANKSGIVING IN THIS COMEDY?

ANSWER: CHICAGO.

THE ELEPHANT MAN (1980)

WHO PLAYS JOHN MERRICK, THE SEVERELY DEFORMED MAN, IN THIS BIOGRAPHICAL DRAMA?

ANSWER: JOHN HURT.

TERMS OF ENDEARMENT (1983)

WHAT IS THE NAME OF AURORA GREENWAY'S DAUGHTER, PLAYED BY DEBRA WINGER?

ANSWER: EMMA HORTON.

FERRIS BUELLER'S DAY OFF (1986)

WHAT IS THE NAME OF THE HIGH SCHOOL
THAT FERRIS, CAMERON, AND SLOANE
ATTEND IN THE FILM?

ANSWER: SHERMER HIGH SCHOOL.

TOOTSIE (1982)

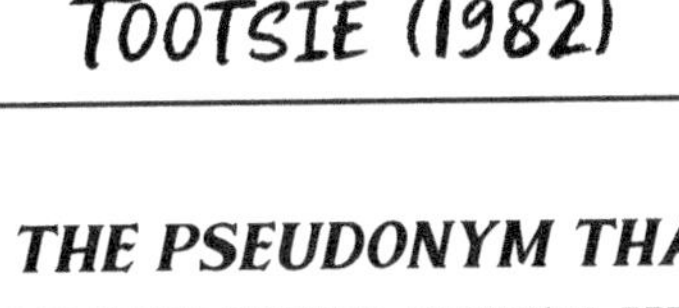

WHAT IS THE PSEUDONYM THAT ACTOR MICHAEL DORSEY USES WHEN HE DISGUISES HIMSELF AS A WOMAN TO GET A ROLE?

ANSWER: DOROTHY MICHAELS.

THE LAST EMPEROR (1987)

WHO PORTRAYS THE TITULAR CHARACTER, PUYI, THE LAST EMPEROR OF CHINA?

ANSWER: JOHN LONE.

SHORT CIRCUIT (1986)

WHAT IS THE NAME OF THE MILITARY ROBOT THAT GAINS HUMAN-LIKE CONSCIOUSNESS IN THIS SCI-FI COMEDY?

ANSWER: NUMBER 5 (OR JOHNNY FIVE).

GREMLINS (1984)

WHAT IS THE NAME OF THE MAIN MOGWAI CHARACTER?

ANSWER: GIZMO.

Ferris Bueller's Day Off (1986)

What is the name of the high school
principal determined to catch
Ferris in the act?

ANSWER: PRINCIPAL ED ROONEY.

The Right Stuff (1983)

What is the nickname given to the first seven American astronauts selected for the space program?

ANSWER: THE MERCURY SEVEN.

THE NEVERENDING STORY (1984)

WHAT IS THE NAME OF ATREYU'S LOYAL
AND WISE HORSE-LIKE COMPANION?

ANSWER: ARTAX.

A Fish Called Wanda (1988)

What is the name of the stuttering, animal-loving character played by Michael Palin?

ANSWER: KEN PILE.

BLUE VELVET (1986)

WHO DIRECTED THIS DARK AND
SURREAL CRIME THRILLER SET IN A
SEEMINGLY IDYLLIC SUBURBAN TOWN?

ANSWER: DAVID LYNCH.

TOP GUN (1986)

WHICH SONG FROM "TOP GUN" WON THE
ACADEMY AWARD FOR BEST ORIGINAL SONG?

ANSWER: TAKE MY BREATH AWAY.

Big Trouble in Little China (1986)

What is the name of the
larger-than-life truck driver
played by Kurt Russell?

ANSWER: JACK BURTON.

THE LAST STARFIGHTER (1984)

IN WHAT ARCADE GAME DOES THE PROTAGONIST ALEX ROGAN EXCEL, LEADING TO AN UNEXPECTED ADVENTURE?

ANSWER: STARFIGHTER.

WarGames (1983)

WHAT IS THE NAME OF THE SUPERCOMPUTER
THAT ALMOST STARTS WORLD WAR III
IN THIS THRILLER?

*ANSWER: WOPR
(WAR OPERATION PLAN RESPONSE).*

BEETLEJUICE (1988)

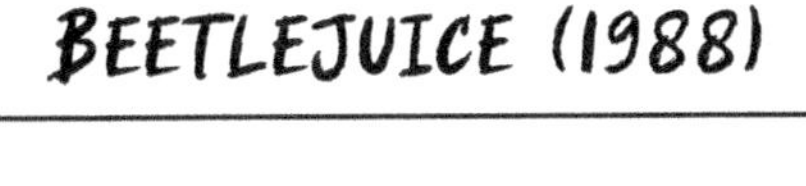

WHAT IS THE NAME OF THE DEETZ FAMILY'S GOTH DAUGHTER, WHO CAN SEE THE MAITLANDS AS GHOSTS?

ANSWER: LYDIA.

Planes, Trains, and Automobiles (1987)

What item does Neal Page mistakenly leave behind at a gas station early in his journey?

ANSWER: HIS WALLET.

THE LOST BOYS (1987)

WHAT IS THE NAME OF THE VAMPIRE GANG'S LEADER, PLAYED BY KIEFER SUTHERLAND?

ANSWER: DAVID.

The Breakfast Club (1985)

What does the "S" in Brian Johnson's sandwich lunchbox stand for?

ANSWER: SUSHI.

Back to the Future Part II (1989)

In what year does Marty McFly travel to in this sequel to the original "Back to the Future"?

ANSWER: 2015.

The Terminator (1984)

What is the model number of ther terminator played by Arnold Schwarzenegger?

ANSWER: THE T-800.

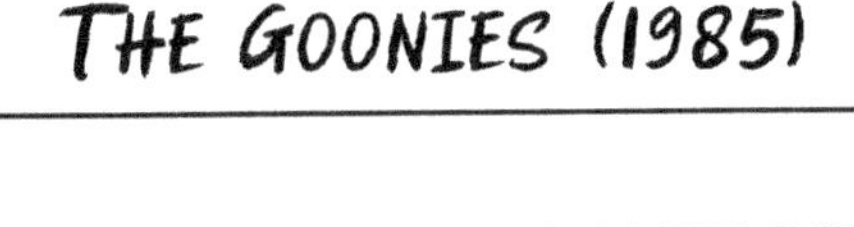

THE GOONIES (1985)

WHAT IS THE NAME OF THE PIRATE SHIP THE KIDS DISCOVER AT THE END OF THEIR ADVENTURE?

ANSWER: THE INFERNO.

Stand By Me (1986)

Which author wrote the novel that "Stand by Me" is based on?

ANSWER: STEPHEN KING.

GREMLINS (1984)

*WHAT THREE RULES MUST BE FOLLOWED
WHEN CARING FOR A MOGWAI,
ACCORDING TO MR. WING?*

*ANSWER: KEEP THEM AWAY FROM BRIGHT
LIGHT, DON'T GET THEM WET,
AND NEVER FEED THEM AFTER MIDNIGHT.*

TOP GUN (1986)

WHAT IS THE CALL SIGN OF
MAVERICK'S WINGMAN AND
BEST FRIEND IN THE MOVIE?

ANSWER: GOOSE.

Dirty Dancing (1987)

What is the name of the resort where Baby and her family spend their summer vacation?

ANSWER: KELLERMAN'S.

THE KARATE KID (1984)

*WHAT IS THE SIGNATURE MOVE
THAT MR. MIYAGI TEACHES
DANIEL TO DEFEND HIMSELF?*

ANSWER: THE CRANE KICK.

THE TERMINATOR (1984)

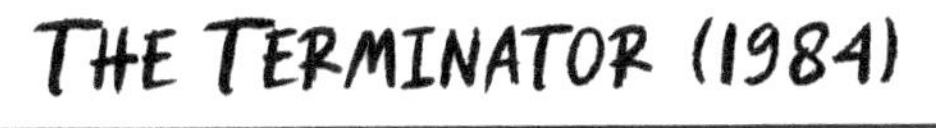

WHAT IS THE NAME OF SARAH CONNOR'S
UNBORN SON, WHO BECOMES THE
FUTURE SAVIOR OF HUMANITY?

ANSWER: JOHN CONNOR.

PLATOON (1986)

WHO PLAYS THE MORALLY CONFLICTED
SOLDIER CHRIS TAYLOR IN THIS
VIETNAM WAR DRAMA?

ANSWER: CHARLIE SHEEN.

RAIDERS OF THE LOST ARK (1981)

**WHAT ANCIENT ARTIFACT IS
INDIANA JONES TRYING TO FIND
BEFORE THE NAZIS IN THIS FILM?**

ANSWER: THE ARK OF THE COVENANT.

The Little Mermaid (1989)

What does Ursula steal from Ariel, which leads to her transformation into a human?

ANSWER: HER VOICE.

The Empire Strikes Back (1980

What character loses a hand
during a lightsaber duel in
this Star Wars sequel?

ANSWER: LUKE SKYWALKER.

THE NEVERENDING STORY (1984)

WHAT IS THE NAME OF THE YOUNG
HERO OF THE STORY WHO READS
THE MAGICAL BOOK?

ANSWER: BASTIAN.

The Shining (1980)

What is the name of the eerie, haunted hotel where the story takes place?

ANSWER: THE OVERLOOK HOTEL.

FIRST BLOOD (1982)

IN WHICH FICTIONAL TOWN DOES THE CONFLICT BETWEEN JOHN RAMBO AND THE LOCAL POLICE TAKE PLACE?

ANSWER: HOPE, WASHINGTON.

E.T. THE EXTRA-TERRESTRIAL (1982)

WHAT DOES ELLIOTT USE TO COMMUNICATE
WITH E.T. AND HELP HIM BUILD
A DEVICE TO "PHONE HOME"?

ANSWER: A SPEAK & SPELL.

THE GOONIES (1985)

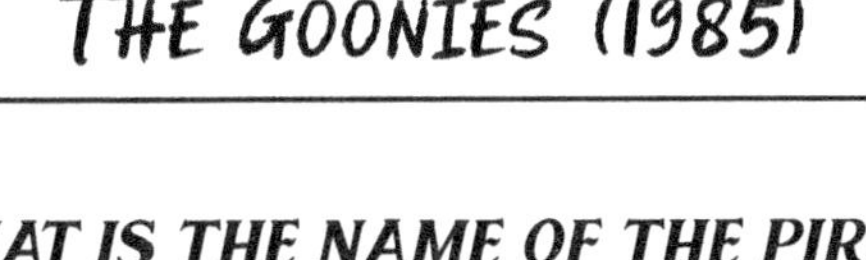

WHAT IS THE NAME OF THE PIRATE WHOSE TREASURE THE KIDS ARE SEARCHING FOR IN THIS ADVENTURE FILM?

ANSWER: ONE-EYED WILLY.

The Outsiders (1983)

Who wrote the novel "The Outsiders," on which the film is based?

ANSWER: S.E. HINTON.

THE COLOR PURPLE (1985)

WHAT IS THE NAME OF THE
ABUSIVE HUSBAND WHO
TORMENTS CELIE IN THE FILM?

ANSWER: ALBERT (MISTER).

LABYRINTH (1986)

*WHO PLAYS JARETH,
THE GOBLIN KING, IN THIS
FANTASY MUSICAL?*

ANSWER: DAVID BOWIE.

E.T. THE EXTRA-TERRESTRIAL (1982)

WHAT TYPE OF CANDY DOES ELLIOTT USE TO LURE E.T. INTO HIS HOUSE?

ANSWER: REESE'S PIECES.

BACK TO THE FUTURE (1985)

WHAT SPEED MUST THE DeLOREAN REACH TO ENABLE TIME TRAVEL?

ANSWER: 88 MILES PER HOUR.

GHOSTBUSTERS (1984)

WHO ARE THE FOUR MAIN GHOSTBUSTERS IN THE ORIGINAL MOVIE?

ANSWER: PETER VENKMAN, RAY STANTZ,
EGON SPENGLER, AND WINSTON ZEDDEMORE.

DIE HARD (1988)

WHAT IS THE NAME OF THE
BUILDING WHERE THE HOSTAGE
SITUATION TAKES PLACE?

Answer: Nakatomi Plaza.

ROBOCOP (1987)

IN WHICH FUTURISTIC CITY IS THE MOVIE SET?

ANSWER: DETROIT, MICHIGAN.

The Karate Kid (1984)

What is the name of the teenager
who moves to California and learns
karate from Mr. Miyagi?

ANSWER: DANIEL LARUSSO.

We hope you thoroughly enjoyed the book and found it both engaging and informative. Your feedback is invaluable to us, and we would greatly appreciate it if you could take a moment to rate the book online.

Additionally, for more fun and challenging quizzes, visit our YouTube page at "Reel Knowledge Riddles." There, you will find a variety of content designed to test your knowledge and entertain you.

Thank you for your support!